Paradigm Shift

Paradigm Shift

Poems by

Judith Rosner

Second edition.
First published in 2025; second edition published in 2026.

© 2025, 2026 Judith Rosner. All rights reserved.
This material may not be reproduced in any form, published,
reprinted, recorded, performed, broadcast,
rewritten, or redistributed without
the explicit permission of Judith Rosner.
All such actions are strictly prohibited by law.

Cover design by Shay Culligan
Cover photo by Judith Rosner
Author photo by Ira S. Rosner

ISBN: 979-8-90146-904-0
Library of Congress Control Number: 2026938133

Kelsay Books
502 South 1040 East, A-119
American Fork, Utah 84003
Kelsaybooks.com

Acknowledgments

Grateful acknowledgment to the editors of the following publications in which these poems, some in earlier versions, first appeared:

Bards Against Hunger 10 Year Anthology: "Pick Up at P.S. 261"
The City Key: "Waking with the City"
Florida Bards Poetry Anthology 2024: "School of Maine"
Gulf Coast Poets/Florida Bards Poetry Anthology: "Child of My Child"
HerWords: "The Mother I Never Knew," "Who is She?"
The Jewish Writing Project: "From Russia with Love"
Living Peace 2019 Art of Poetry Anthology: "Forest Sanctuary"
Naugatuck River Review: "The Interrogation"

I have been fortunate to have a network of family, friends, fellow poets and writers as supports throughout my writing career. With warm appreciation and thanks to members of my Sarasota poetry community—Allen Smuckler, Mary Saily, Mike Kozubek, Linda Robiner, Abby Karish, Karen Edwards, Greg Gaul, Mark Braaten, Gordon Kuhn, Tanya Young, Barbara Harris, Sara Lazarus, and Barbara Cummings—for your valued feedback and editorial comments. And I am grateful for the friendship and support of both my New York writing group—Betsy Freedman, Cora Hoberman, Debra Banerjee, Suzanne Chait, and Micheline Haas and my Florida writing group—Cheryl Zaccagnino, Diane Arch, Charlotte McPherson, Lorraine Asarch, Risa Marlen, Judith Koziol, and Margaret Goldberger. All of you have encouraged me and helped me strengthen my writing voice over the years.

Many thanks and much appreciation go to Sarah Stern whose sage editing and wise questioning strengthened my poems. A big thank you to Lev Ayalon for his creative suggestions regarding the book's cover. And further appreciation goes to the team at Kelsay Books for help in making this book come to life.

Thank you to my daughter Ari, son-in-law Omri, and grandchildren Lev and Eliana. Your love surrounds me and bolsters me—and you give me grist for the poetry mill. To Skip, my love, my partner in life, thank you for being by my side always.

Contents

Part 3: My world has turned dark

Part 4: Not halved / But doubly whole

Part 5: Line by line

Part 6: What I crave

Part 7: Wonders to know

Part 8: Dance

for Ari

Part 1:

The cocoon in which I grew

From Russia with Love

"Take these candlesticks my child,
And when you light them
in your own home,
Remember me and the family you came from."

My grandmother, a girl of fifteen, heeded her mother
and carried these silver twins, wrapped in a pillowcase,
across the ocean.
She faithfully recited the Sabbath blessing over them
each Friday evening, her family gathered at the table.

Now two generations later, they
still stand tall upon their three-pronged legs
in my home.
Grape vines etched upon their stems

show off clusters of ripened fruit
amid the dings and dents of age and
dark spots where tarnish resists polish.
On this Friday evening, I light them too.

Mom and Dad

The cocoon in which I grew
was smooth on one side,
prickly on the other.
I flourished between them.

His dry sense of humor
        Her wet kisses
His creative bent
        Her legal mind
His common sense
        Her flights of fancy
He reserved
        She gregarious
He the cheerleader
        She the critic
He graduated high school
        She law school
He at the drums
        She at the piano
Playing a duet of opposites.

Father's Teachings

In your shadow I learned to fly.
Your lessons, not preached
but lived, instruct my life still:

Love can be spoken in silence
Giving is the essence of getting
Patience paves the road to success
Listen to what people do, not say.

You gave me strength
as I pursued a degree,
shone light on the child who carries your name,
and twinkle still at my rhymes.

I think of you when I purchase gifts,
when I wrap a package as you taught me,
when I speak love without words.
I miss you, Dad.

Attorney at Law, 1935

Sheet music to “I Did It My Way”
lays open on piano’s music stand.
Her theme song,
testament to how she lived life.

A woman born before her time
but of her time,
Constrained by culture, not by will,
Her pioneer persona in constant conflict
with “good housekeeping” norms.

Perhaps this is why she didn’t want
the same for me, suggesting I follow
a more traditional path,
one that would protect me
from the fire she faced.

No matter. Her spirit gave me strength,
Her life-force imparted spunk and spine,
All qualities I needed to fight
the battles I would confront
as a woman in my own time.

Watermelon

Dad knew the way to pick them.
He told us stories of how,
as a kid in California,
he pulled plugs from their
hard green shells
to reveal ruby red flesh.

At our backyard barbecue,
he'd cut clean, perfect triangles,
delivering them on white fluted paper plates
soggy with the fruit's juices.
We ate at the picnic table covered
in a red and white checked oilcloth.

This fruit, spotted with slippery black seeds,
perfect for my brother and me
to spit at each other,
was a fitting finish
to our charcoal broiled feast.
Licking sticky fingers, we headed to bed.

School of Maine

One week each year our family set off on vacation
from cosmopolitan New York City to foreign territory—
the State of Maine.

Father feared there would be no grocery stores
in the land of forests and bears,
So we travelled weighted down by canned goods
and a well-stocked first aid shoebox
to a housekeeping cottage on Lake Cobbosseecontee.

I was a girl who had her nose in a book most of the time,
And who only knew how to play hop-scotch,
jacks, and pick-up sticks.
This was where I learned to waterski, play ping pong,
and slice a silent lake with a canoe paddle while
I listened to bird songs and the beat of my heart.

It was where I tasted scallops for the first time
served up at the local diner.
Sweet and fried, ready for dipping in tartar sauce—
a treat prohibited in my almost Kosher kitchen.
Maine seemed far enough away to make it feel "okay."

It was where on early mornings I sat with my father in a row boat.
He taught me how to put worms on hooks and cast a line.
In silence, we waited for a tug,
the possibility of a fish,
and the experience of a catch.

It was where I felt the exhilaration of a billowed sail,
And the heat of beating sun when set adrift.
Where I learned that wind can be both friend and foe,
In a flash turning water's surface from glass to gale.
These lessons I learned on Lake Cobbosseecontee.

It was there, on a moonlit night,
On the shore of the Lake,
Snuggled at the base of a birch tree,
I kissed a boy for the first time.
I can't remember his name.

The Sears Roebuck Christmas Gift Catalogue

Nothing heralded the advent of the holiday season
with greater fanfare than when my father brought home
the Sears Roebuck Christmas Gift Catalogue.
I would sit and ponder the pages for hours.

The toys, the pretty girl models in beautiful clothes—
these colorful pictures would invite me
to read their descriptions. The price
would tell me if I had a chance to call
the doll or dress my own.

I knew my father helped create the catalogue.
The page make-up, the layout of the toys' pictures,
the size type used in describing them, were all
decisions in which he had a hand. Reading the catalogue
felt like "take your daughter to work day."

For each of the eight nights of Chanukah,
my parents would give me a shiny,
newly-minted quarter.

On the last night, I also received a present—
like the gray corduroy dress with fancy white buttons,
white collar, and white trim on the sleeves
found on page 192.

Father's Day, 1960

My father was a cotton knit man,
Not a Banlon man.
So when he asked for a shirt for Father's Day
I knew what he wanted.

I took the Q76 bus to Flushing—
a place I was familiar with from shopping
with teenage friends.
I found it was the year of Banlon.

Salesmen in store after store told me
no cotton knit shirts were to be had,
My father was behind the times,
Fashion dictated a new fabric.

I went home giftless. Then I
wrote my father a letter describing
my conversation with each salesman,
Replete with quotes.

I gave him my letter as a present on Father's Day
and was rewarded with laughter.
"This is the best present you could give me,"
he said once he caught his breath.

After he passed away,
I found the letter saved
in his bureau drawer.

The Mother I Never Knew

She looks up at me from the long ago photograph,
Light shining on smooth cheek and stenciled brow,
Smile so genuine, playful, unforced,
Her face framed by wavy hair the color of night.

Could she have always been this lovely,
So unpretentious, and I never noticed?
Was I unable to see beneath the mask,
Beyond my own tinged view of her?

This woman's picture taken
before my time,
Is the mother I never knew
and remember so differently.

Ruthie Stories

I listen to the stand-up comic
tell tales about his alcoholic father.
They are funny. I laugh.

But not for long.

I realize I tell Ruthie stories
about my mother. Friends
even ask for them—they're funny

as long as Ruthie isn't your mother.

The comic and I find ways
to cordon off the hurt,
But it never goes away

even when we laugh with our audience.

The Day After Thanksgiving, 1971

It was a quiet Thanksgiving—
both of us children were away,
So our parents decided to work on Friday.

Rather than ride the bus and subway,
they treated themselves to
tickets on the Long Island Railroad.

With a "Bye Babe" and "See you, Hon,"
they kissed goodbye at Penn Station and
agreed to meet for the 5:40 train home.

At ten that morning, my mother
received a call from my father's office,
"There was nothing we could do, Ruth . . ."

I stare out plane's window unseeing,
my body limp, heart wrung dry,
and fly home to a mother in disbelief,
repeating the story over and over.

I find my father's chair empty,
an uneven number for dinner,
one fewer plate at the table.

She's Gone

Her raised eyebrow once
spoke paragraphs.
Her sneer shook my world.

Eyes that caught my tiniest flaws
now stare through me. Eyes,
she said, she had at the back of her head.

Her lips barely move
to smile or speak, countenance
unable to glower or glow.

Her face once a palette
of expression wiped clean
by illness and age,

I realize how much
I miss my mother
and how she spoke to me.

Treasure Trove

She stands in the corner off to one side
Not very tall and not very wide
Her four legs somewhat shaky and thin
Her importance—what's held within.

Her top drops down with a squeak at the joint
(Not unlike bending my knees at this point)
Revealing cubbyhole compartments dense
With riches galore, all in past tense.

Here are loving letters in Dad's careful hand,
There are pictures of Mom and me in the sand.
And notes from my brother when I was away
Telling tales of home life and keeping girls at bay.

Grandma and Grandpa appear in a snap,
Could that be two-year-old me in one's lap?
Awards and medals and things of the like
Sidle up next to pic of brother on trike.

Mom's student desk, private treasure trove
Waits for whenever I need through it rove.
Its contents wrap me fast in family fold,
Bring me close to those I miss, long to hold.

Scents of Autumn

Autumn dips into her pockets,
Flings coins of red and gold at upturned leaves.
Crisp air, crunchy as a bite of apple, complements color.

Soon skies will silver, send sleet and rain
to slap leaves to ground. This is
the season of my parents' deaths.

I pray over memorial candles in my kitchen.
Above their waxy smoke, memories of
childhood smells mingle with scents of the season.

I recall the spice of Father's aftershave
as he leaned in to kiss me "good morning"
on his way out the door,

the bouquet of Mother's signature perfume,
Estee Lauder's Youth Dew, that would signal
her entrance,

the odor of rubber cement on Father's fingers,
and the mouth-watering whiff of Mother's
pot roast simmering on the stove at dinner time.

These memories of childhood smells
make me long for parents—a yearning only
relieved when a new season opens her arms to me.

Part 2:

The speaker of soft words

Beshert: Meant to Be

He sat behind the check-in desk,
Blue eyes twinkling, sporting a
“Let me in” smile.
Dressed in jacket and tie,
He owned the space around him.
We chatted and joked for a while,
Both of us aware of the chemistry.

Driving Lessons

I had no idea how hard it was to turn a steering wheel,
nudge around a corner,
orchestrate the movement of my feet
on three pedals—make the monster move.

My teacher was patient with me,
deciding I'd do less damage starting
in a chair rather than behind
the wheel of the first car he ever owned.

Three shoes faced me: sneaker, slipper, sandal.
"Now," he said, "when you put your foot down on the sandal,
you come up on the sneaker." And to give me full effect,
he mimicked engine's sound so I'd think I was moving.

What love!

To learn to turn, he took me to an empty parking lot
where he had me execute figure eights around barrels
over and over again looking for perfection.
This gave me a splitting headache and I was angry.

I married him anyway.

Open to Love

You cracked my shell.
No longer would witty come-backs
or sassy sarcasm serve to
fend off possible hurt,
rejection, loss.
You told me I didn't need armor,
that I was enough.

So I breathed in the fresh air
of freedom to just be me.
From you, I learned that love
most easily lands on a soft heart.

The Interrogation

He stood at the door of my parents' home
holding a small black box.
It was my eighteenth birthday. His gifts—
Himself and a blue star sapphire drop necklace.

My mother said, "Give it back. It's too expensive."
What she meant: "This is too serious a gift from a boy
who's only known my young daughter a short time."

Three years later, I was still wearing my sapphire necklace
when he stood at my parents' door.
One look at my face and he knew I hadn't told them
we were planning to marry after my college graduation.

He stayed cloistered in my bedroom upstairs while I
informed my parents in the living room.
"This is hitting me like a ton of bricks," Mom said.

An attorney, she was skilled at cross-examination.
As her daughter, I knew preparation was key
when I'd have to take the stand.
I was ready.

Then, with barely a pause, the questions—
What will you live on? Where will you live?
What about graduate school?

My father, quiet through this give and take,
"While your mother catches her breath,
I just want you to know that we wish you
all the happiness in the world."

Lucky Charm

I slip my hand ’round the cup’s smooth surface
and drink my coffee from it each morning.
While coffee wakes me, the vessel sustains.
Half century ago, a friend of Diane’s offered to house
me the evening before I defended my dissertation.

She sensed my anxiety and understood
the importance of my mission.
On the morning of the ordeal she
presented me with a gift, a lucky charm.

A cricket dances on each of the cup’s sides—
Creature of good luck whose wisdom
speaks to joy, intuition, power of belief—
A daily reminder of my good fortune.

Who Is She?

She's the speaker of soft words,
The smoother of ruffled feathers,
Filing sharp edges, removing judgment,
Making criticism easier to digest.

She's the monkey in the middle,
The mediator listening with
an ear to each side,
Helping to reach resolution.

But injustice served on her
scratches that smooth surface.
Her voice, assertive and calm,
Speaks fighting words of reason.

She surprises others with her tenacity
to seek truth, make fair the inequity,
Promote flex in a rigid system,
Rewrite rules in light of new evidence.

Soft words are difficult to hear
over the din of "what's always been done,"
So she chooses battles wisely
and quietly, firmly, becomes agent of change.

For Robert M. O'Shea

I searched for you, I did,
And came up with naught
until your picture and obituary
filled my computer's screen.
Your blue eyes twinkled through the photo
and your slight smile seemed meant just for me.
I've wanted to thank you for clearing the way,
For laying the first bricks of my career path.

But I let a few hurts get in the way—
Cancelled appointments, late responses,
the last-minute change of my dissertation
defense date—all seem like minor offenses
now that I view them through older eyes.
Please accept my prayers of gratitude
as they now soar to you.

Sunlight's Magic

Her rays slip under bedroom shades
cancelling dreams, waking the world to day.
Her glance on morning dew dresses
each blade of grass in chemise of rainbow hues,
And with a toss of her head, she turns
leaden buildings to gleaming armored soldiers.

When she flies her wand across the waves,
Stars of white dance on every ripple.
When she shines through forest dark,
A dappled path's revealed.
And when she kisses your cheek just so,
I see the boy I married so very long ago.

Quiet Love

Yes, there is the rough and tumble love,
the wild "I must have you love,"
But quiet love often
moves me more.

Quiet love, the love that's shared holding hands
exploring a new trail by day,
ambling familiar streets at night after a play.
The quiet love shared sitting on a bench listening to birds,
or the glances passed when our child says or does
something that moves us the same way.

The quiet love that comes from discovering foreign lands,
tasting new foods, lifting glasses of wine to
toast my edited poem, your improved tennis.
The quiet love that comes from doing for the other
what is wanted, but never asked for.

The quiet love is wild, wonderful—you.

For Ari on Her 36th Birthday

Light glows where you walk
And shines brighter when you smile
Igniting my heart.

Reasons

10 Reasons to Text

Because there's no time for a call.
Because you're in a meeting.
So that I don't have to answer the question, "How are you?"
Because I know you won't listen to a voicemail.
Because I'm on the subway.
So that you won't hear the crack in my voice.
So that I don't have to listen to your answer to, "How are you?"
Because I don't want to hear the clack of your computer while you pretend to listen.
Because you'll respond to a text, but not answer a call.
So that you won't hear how tired I sound.

10 Reasons to Call

Because I want to hear you laugh.
Because the song your voice sings is one I'll never tire of.
Because it's been so long since we've spoken.
Because I have time to listen.
Because a chat with you brightens my day.
Because your voice will tell me how you're really feeling.
Because I truly want to see you, and calling is the next best thing.
Because you have a way of quelling my fears.
So that I can run down an agenda of things I need answers to.
Because the extraneous versus the pith is often the most telling.

Gilvan's Department Store, Warwick, NY

More than a store, Gilvan's was the center, our town's lifeforce—
Mike, the beating heart behind the counter.
He was mayor, chamber president, cog in the wheel
that was Warwick—though these titles weren't really his.

Gilvan's had clothing for the whole family on the racks
and shelves lining her three floors. She was a century old;
her bricks spoke of character, her staircase and curved banister
proudly transported you up and down her spine.

In a world without internet, Gilvan's was better than Google Meet.
Here was a physical space where news was shared, gossip spread,
Where, as an exhausted new mother, I could visit
knowing both my daughter and I would score a break.

Mike would swoop Ari into his arms and take her next door
to the greasy spoon diner where they would share rice pudding
or babble over a bowl of rum raisin ice cream,
leaving me free to shop or talk with friends and neighbors.

Pearl, Mike's wife and Gilvan's buyer, made sure not to
purchase too many of one dress since we were all invited
to the same parties. She knew who looked good in what,
Who needed clothes for work, the ages of everyone's children.

Gilvan's building on Main Street still lingers,
But her soul resides in the hearts of her patrons,
Who along with clothing, laughter and even childcare,
Found friendship when passing through her doors.

Part 3:

My world has turned dark

COVID Arrives

Masked and gloved,
We walk six feet apart.
Hard to hold hands,
Feel a smile.
Our eyes speak for us:
fear, resignation, hope
All at the same time.

From our isolated posts
We watch as politicians' egos
Deflate like overblown balloons
In light of science, not rhetoric,
Data, not distraction,
Death toll in numbers too great.

A COVID monarchy rules the world.
Our enemy a crowned microbe,
A virus spreading to rich and poor,
Young and old, right and left.
It knows no boundaries,
Speaks the same language
in whatever country it conquers.

Navigating in Strange Times

Adrift, unmoored, and rudderless,
I search for a place to land,
Somewhere to be, someone to see,
Wanting, waiting to be anchored,
Feel safe, secure, but free.

Best, I think, to travel inward,
Not seek port outside myself.
Sail instead on secret channels
hidden deep 'tween heart and mind.
Hitch my line to buried talents,
Draw on canvas now revealed,
Write on pages empty, open,
Eager for my thoughts, my dreams.

What I Learned While Sheltering in Place

I enjoy a walk with my husband as much as a walk with a friend.
The things I thought I'd do if I had time, aren't things I want to do.
No need to leave voicemails—everyone is home!
Some affix "elderly" to me. I don't like it.
My husband and I can work well in the kitchen together.
There are a lot of people who care about me.
I need structure more than I realized.
I must have a calendar of places to be to know what day it is.
Changing linen, making beds, doing wash take on project prominence.
Parkinson's Law applies to me—my work expands to fill the time available.
How to use Zoom to connect to others and to learn new things.
I can listen to Jazz from Lincoln Center for free.
I can spend more time with my grandchildren on FaceTime—
and read a book upside down to them so they can see the pictures.
I'm not motivated to write or start projects. I'm best with a deadline.
A trip to Publix or Costco can be the bright spot in a day.
Amazon boxes at the door bring joy—even if they're vitamins.

In This World

In this world of nowhere to be
No one to see,

I wake to birdsong rhapsody,
A pre-dawn reveille, and watch
As breeze blows mist away
To greet a brand-new day.

In this world of nowhere to be
No one to see,

Children check in to learn
If I'm feeling okay,
Screen play with little ones
A joy I look forward to each day.

In this world of nowhere to be
No one to see,

Friends call from far-off ports
To ask how I'm faring.
Catching up on years we've missed,
Brings us close together again.

In this world of nowhere to be
No one to see,

I walk 'long nature's trails,
Follow river, plant and bird,
Enjoy trees' shade, not
Knowing where path ends.

In this world of nowhere to be
No one to see,

I've learned to linger over dinner,
Enjoy soft pink sunset skies,
And this quiet gives me time,
Time to meditate, to think, to write.

In this world of nowhere to be
No one to see,

I miss the hugs of family,
The sight and touch of friends
As we chat over coffee
At our favorite café.

In this world of nowhere to be
No one to see,

I miss the hubbub of busy restaurants,
The tension of an audience's
Anticipation before the curtain lifts,
The joy of live performance.

In this world of nowhere to be
No one to see,

I miss the travel to foreign shores
To see new sights,
Meet new people,
Delight in learning of their lives.

Should all I've missed return one day,
I hope to keep the tranquil grace
I've treasured,
Living through . . .

This world of nowhere to be
No one to see.

Outdoor Theater, 2020

The brown-green moss sways with the breeze
like a chorus line kicking in tune to music.
Mocking bird mimics his way through a solo
while doves, his backup singers, coo along.
Now cardinal sweeps in for a cameo appearance
and I applaud with a smile and a nod to the stage.

Summer Breeze, 2020

It is dusk, soft evening breezes
sweep away day's heat,
tickle the hibiscus whose
petals have closed for the night.

I want to feel the garden's calm,
But the erratic clink-clink
of neighbor's chimes rattles
my already jangled nerves,

reminds me of unfinished business,
plans halted mid-stream,
children far out of reach,
health held in a liar's hands.

I realize as day loses light,
Peace will not visit me tonight.

November, 2020

It’s Saturday after the election.
The warmth and light of sun’s rays
so rare on a November New York City day
belies the mood, the tense air
almost visibly vibrating off
masked walkers like me
trying to ease the unease by moving.

Shouts in the distance disrupt—
Another protest? Possible riot?
But no, the noise is joyous.
It flows in waves across avenues, between streets.
People pop out from open windows
cheering, banging pots, ringing bells.
Horns honk, hands wave from buses, cars, delivery vans.

I clap, cheer, shout, with my fellow New Yorkers who
spill to the sidewalk, leaving brunch at the table.
The relief is palpable. I taste the salt of
tears released without my realizing,
Shedding tension, embracing joy,
Celebrating the Biden-Harris election.

View from the FDR Drive During COVID

New York City is dressed up tonight.
Pearl necklaces hang from her bridges
over the East River whose water shines bright
under a moon so full it's blinding.

Apartment buildings look like happy robots
as windows blink on and off in tune to jazz
playing on the car radio. The Empire State Building
glows sapphire blue.

My spirit soars this evening
knowing my city stays strong
through tough times, and even
dresses up when there's no place to go.

Speed Bump in the Time of COVID

The world has hit a speed bump,
A liminal space,
A neutral zone,
A saddle on the threshold of new.

We know this side of the bump,
Its prejudices, class struggles,
Crises of climate, guns, virus,
isolation, a country divided.

Time to fashion a new world.

The speed bump's jolt should
slow us down, wake us up.
But will it?

A Prayer

Let's leave last year's words behind us—
Pandemic, COVID, ventilators, loneliness, and loss
And welcome new words in a new voice
Singing songs of hope, reassurance and joy.

Enough

on the eve of the November, 2022 elections

Enough jabbering negatives
And talking in circles
About things red and blue
And turning to purple.

Enough lies and defenses
Pollsters and pundits
Pessimistic ponderings
During dinner discussions.

Enough ads and campaigns
Emails and leaflets
Requests for donations
For one or another.

But enough of this patter
Is never enough
If we want to be heard
Want our voices to matter.

Lost Light

after the shooting at the Tree of Life Synagogue in Pittsburgh

My world has turned dark.
No sun peeks through the walls of hate
to paint the country of my dreams.
All colors vanished, banished.

I miss the warmth of yellow and red,
The joy pink speaks, the violet of hope.
I miss the green of living things
growing strong in earthen brown.

I even long for shades of gray
where understanding resides
and listening is key
to light again this land of mine.

In Response to Jackson Pollack's *Convergence*

Messy movement,
Swirls of black and white,
Splotches of yellow tinged in red,
Lines asquiggle marking paths
ending nowhere.

The world today,
Black and white,
Spotted by bloodshed,
No hint of yellow to
point a path forward.

Part 4:

Not halved / But doubly whole

Snowbird

The compass spins
Where will it land
At sooted window north
Or sunny one due south

Where buses fart
And people bustle
Or where herons fly
And fish play catch

Where family thrives
And "Grandma play" is heard
Or where birds call greetings
And wildlife abounds

Where Broadway beams
And museums enchant
Or where life lays back
And beaches beckon

Where horns honk
To a Manhattan mantra
Or where quiet prevails
Among palms and ponds

Each place tugs
With its enticements
But when settled in one
I let go the other.

My world not halved
But doubly whole.

A New York Moment

It's summer and I sunbathe
on a bench in Riverside Park.
A man practicing the saxophone
faces away from me playing as he looks
out at traffic along the West Side Highway.

While others catch a few notes as they walk by,
I stay for the whole concert.
My bench is behind him, so I'm not sure
he knows he has an audience of one—
privileged to have a front row seat.

When he packs up and turns to leave
I walk toward him to tell him
how much I enjoyed his playing.
He's turned toward me to let me know
he's sorry if he disturbed me.

I learn he's an editor—
the saxophone a release from words.
"I wrote a poem while you played," I tell him,
"Your music released my words."

Hallelujah Man

He is a tall brown man in a long brown coat
sporting a black fedora
every day and in every kind of weather.
His most distinguishing characteristic—his voice.
It's powerful, sonorous, reverential,
and he uses it to share only one word—"Hallelujah!"

He's a neighborhood fixture
who chants his mantra, his hymn
inviting us pagans on the sidewalk
into the sanctuary he carries on his shoulders.
While he holds pamphlets, he only hands one over
if you approach him.

"Hallelujah!"

His voice rises above honks and hollers,
sirens and buses.
I look forward to his rounding the corner of 106th Street—
often when I'm preparing dinner. I hear him first,
then see him through my kitchen window,
and I feel blessed.

City Birder

From my third-floor window
I choose not to peer at traffic,
not to focus on boarded windows
and ugly signs across the street.

Instead, I gaze into the tree clothed
in a dress of slender green leaves
growing from a square of earth
cut into the sidewalk below.

She opens her skinny arms
beckoning me to look more closely.
I do, and spot a bird's nest
resting askew 'tween trunk and branch.

I need no binoculars, need not strain
as grounded birdwatchers must.
My kitchen window is a perfect perch
from which to watch my winged city friends.

Silence Speaks

Dragonflies dance to the music water makes
as it falls off rock into the creek.

I see the dance, hear the music,
and feel the strength of the rock
beneath me where I sit meditating
in Central Park's North Woods.

Birds of different feather twitter in unison
sounding like an aviary tower of Babel.
Leaves drop quietly one by one,
presaging the approach of a cooler season.

Can you, my comrades in nature,
See my thoughts
Hear my silence
Feel my peace?

The Subway Stranger in Blue Scrubs

She sat across from me,
One of the few riders not bopping to music
flowing from phone through earbuds.
I read exhaustion in her eyes, noticed
her shoulders sagging in an upside-down smile.
I thought of the pain she must have witnessed,
the hands she held, the good news, the bad
she delivered over her shift.

At next stop, mother with toddler entered the car.
The stranger's eyes met mine as we watched
the little one transcend subway travel,
play with imaginary friends in her make-believe world
oblivious to the jumble of people around her.
The stranger and I smiled at each other
as we took in this scene.

When the subway screeched to its next stop,
the stranger rose. I looked up, and
waved as she headed for the door.
She returned a nod as if to say, "Nice to meet you."
Strangers no more.

Let's NOT Do Lunch

Why must "Let's do lunch" follow a greet?
What's wrong with right now and taking a seat?
Other options abound I'm sure as can be,
A walk around town or a sit by the sea.

Or how about biking, hiking, and such
It beats all those calories and eating too much.
Or taking an exercise class to build power
Then lift glass with flexed muscle at Happy Hour.

Or what about just connecting by phone
So we can dress any way and relax in our home.
There's always the choice to leave with a "Ciao,"
'Cause speaking again isn't needed right now.

Fickle Florida Clouds

You'd think they were placed there precisely
by a Hollywood set designer.
Luminous, mirroring sun's shine,
they hang perfectly draped
over the horizon.

Then, without warning, a gusty gray
cloud moves in with menace, threatens rage.
Thunder's trumpet blows in tune
to wind's bluster as the looming cloud
lets free its load dowsing all below.

Like people who turn dark in a flash
and shower you with unkind words
when you least expect.

I learned what would trigger
a torrent from Mother.
In this way I kept the storm at bay.

On the Pond

Mother turtle strains her neck,
Checks right and left for danger,
Finds the place she's found before
to dig her nest, lay eggs in manger.

Her nest's been watched by more than me,
Newly-raided—by crows, I'm sure.
Eggs cracked open, in disarray,
This Spring's turtle babes no more.

Mother duck proudly paddles
as seven ducklings follow her way.
I watch her teach, huddle them close,
Yet shorter grows the line each day.

Hibiscus plant flaunts her blooms,
Pink petals open, gaze at sun.
Hungry bunny catches their glow
and nibbles petals one by one.

While city folk fight for space,
Jockey for jobs, breathe polluted air,
Creature and flower face battles too.
On pond, as in city, not all are spared.

The Hummingbirds

Hung above an arch in Blue Gallery
on the main drag in Delray,
the painting captured me.

Then it spoke.
"Hope" whispered the sky, the color of spring's new leaves,
"Dance" said the birds,
"Dazzle" suggested the silver and gold leaf earth.

The painting was meant for me.
So when I heard it say,
"Take me home,"
I did.

New Year Bird Call

Like birds, I migrate south in winter.
This year I got here first.
The pond was silent.
Not a ripple from a family of ducks,
Not a footprint in the sand of a wading bird.
My only guest, a small blue heron marching to and fro.
He was guarding the place.

But this New Year's Eve morning brought a clamor—
the caws of cranes, the quacks of ducks,
and the tap, tap, tapping of a couple of woodpeckers
on a Christmas palm all sounded reveille.
Relieved, I plan to ring in the new year with them.

Part 5:

Line by line

Dry Spell

The pond's hairline is receding,
Water so low that birds tiptoe on sand
long before they can wade.

Turtle heads pop through pond's surface
startled to see sun so soon.
Air is heavy with promise.

As the pond longs for drink,
a drought of words leaves me thirsty as well.
I sit on the shore, pen in hand,
and wait for words to rain.

Inside Voice

When daughter's children yell too loudly,
She says, "Use your inside voice."
My inside voice is in my head
and I'm the only one who hears the talk,
the constant chatter of conversations
with myself or with another.

I ask, "What needs doing?"
"Whose birthday did I forget?"
I fashion arguments with those I've clashed,
Words I should have said but didn't
to folks I love and those I don't
all rattle 'round inside my head.

My inside voice has written letters, rarely sent.
I chat with friends, no longer with me.
But the words that give such pleasure
are ones that leave my inside voice
and find themselves upon the page
where you may hear them with
the voice inside *your* head.

Dreaming Awake

Come early evening
a shaft of sunlight makes its way
through study window, its shape
informed by city grime upon the panes.

Dust motes dancing on sunbeams
tap out messages from family long gone
as my mind, unbound by time,
plays scenes from an imagined future.

Home Base

When my mind swims
with ideas and asks questions,
When my stomach flutters
with anticipation,
I search for pen and pad,
write and rewrite,
scratch and edit, struggle
with word, form and phrase,
I talk to the world
I talk to myself
I am myself
Here, at home base.

Dolphin Watch

From my seat on the sand, I catch sight of dolphins
and watch as their arched, sun-glittered gray backs
appear, then dip and dive out of view,

their bodies rising and falling with poise and polish.
Playful, too, tails slapping water with friends
as they gather fish for dinner.

I wish I could swim with grace in a sea of words
and assemble them as playfully.
For dolphins a meal, for me a poem.

Lifting Memory's Fog

Fog makes haze of the view
from my window.
Palms faintly outlined
in morning's mist.
Yet squirrels frolic
near where I stand,
Sharply in my sight.

Like my memory these days

The fog will lift
when sun streaks through
and the Monet palette
I feast on now
will lose its mystery,
as writing will uncloud
what once was difficult to see.

He's Back

He's lurking there in a crevice.
Oh, how long he can wait before peeking out,
Longer than I can stand.
I tell him, "You don't have to make a big splash,
A toe in the water will do."
Sometimes he listens.
Flowers bloom when his ideas meet mine.
But he's often selfish, stingy,
Stays a stranger to me.

Wait! I woke with words in my head.
Welcome back, Muse. I'm writing again.

Yearning

I long to blossom in this year's beginning,
To taste the fruit that's been maturing
line by line, stanza by stanza,
to see it take form in my hands.

Part 6:

What I crave

You asked

what I’d like for my birthday.
No gifts that can be touched or bought.
Experiences are what I crave.
To see a new place, taste a new food
and enjoy your company while doing so.
I ask for a new day of exploration with you.

Evening Safari

Under the black-blue African sky
splashed with bright white stars,
six silent people sit in an open jeep.
They wait for the tracker's light
to flash on a pair of animal eyes
as it ping-pongs across the dirt road.

They hope to see a leopard
before going back to cities
where murky gray skies and
streetlights hide heaven's beauty
and where squirrels, not leopards,
cross their paths.

Forest Sanctuary

We shed city's skin to enter forest sanctuary—
an island surrounded by metropolis
but free of its noise, stink, traffic, crowds.
The beating of drums the only sound from without
announcing the commencement of a Buddhist ceremony.

We walk along sun-dappled paths through trees so old
and so tall, their stories so long, we feel insignificant.
Corkscrew vines hang from their branches like Tarzan rope swings
and tree roots, like spider veins, run rampant along our path
ready to trip us as we look skyward at birds alien to our eyes.

Young lovers on bench turn shyly from one another as we pass.
They nod in greeting and we, much older lovers, smile in return.
Following the sound of a sudden rustle of leaves, we come
face to face with a mouse deer as surprised to see us as we him.
We apologize for disturbing his morning ablutions.

Like a temple of and to nature, this refuge exists
as a peaceful haven where prayers of all living things
may be voiced without words and heard without judgment.

The Secret

Tucked away on a Sri Lankan hillside sits
a former British tea baron's bungalow called *The Secret.*
It's now a guesthouse for travelers seeking quiet
disturbed only by starling songs, squirrel scratches,
and monkey howls.

I sit in a garden courtyard looking out at tea plant-carpeted
mountains that fold in and out of one another
as clouds, bruised gray, graze their peaks, threaten rain,
but never fulfill that promise.

This milieu a welcome respite
from a day of climbing mountains and exploring ruins.
I am at peace now, happy to share *The Secret* with you.

Jungle Shower, Sri Lanka

Jostled and tossed, we travel in open-sided safari jeep
along deeply rutted roads, like lines on a leathered face.
My companions bounce, binoculars in hand, cameras at the ready
for the sight of a rare bird, bathing water buffalo, sleeping leopard.
And I, tired of their obsession with getting the perfect shot,
Am unhappy about not being able to enjoy the moment.

Without warning, a passing cloud opens and showers us
with soft rain. While my jeep-mates grumble,
I breathe deep the air once dusty, now sweet and fresh.
Tree trunks turn from dull to glossy brown
and dry grasses, sopping up water like sponges, glow green.

Nothing really can capture this jungle shower,
But the kiss of its raindrops lightened my spirit,
And memory of the moment
stays with me still.

Garden Repose, Kyoto Japan

I walk on colored rocks of varying shape
Along a path leading through flower and shrub
Past a tapestry of trees in multi shades of green
Mirrored in placid pools where painted carp swim.
I see mountains that seem to float
On clouds of pink azalea blooming full in front of me
Hiding the busy, bustling, cramped city below.

A tatami matted teahouse tucked between bowing bamboo
Invites me to remove my shoes and rest a while.
Listening to the silence, the quiet, my mind lets go
Thoughts that rattle and roll, run and rerun
Keeping me from enjoying many moments like this.
My mind space now fills with these Japanese gardens,
Memory-imbedded, ready for retrieval when needed.

Message Sent

The gong hangs high on the platform,
solid, heavy, commanding
at the Shinto shrine's center,
ready to be awakened
by believers with wishes on their lips.

I think of my daughter heavy with child
as I climb to gong's station,
lift the mallet,
put strength behind my strike,
and whisper prayers for a safe delivery.

The sound is low, thick, primitive,
vibrating to the gods.

The Photographer and the Vietnamese Woman

She watched him pointing his camera at the bridge,
Snapping photos of women washing laundry in the river,
Fishermen on stilts throwing nets, children playing on the shore.
He, a tourist, who took a turn on an untrampled path
to capture Vietnamese village life and take home gifts
most would miss, caught by his camera's eye . . .

like the old woman seated on a bench watching him.

Gray wisps rimmed her face, a face leathered
by age and sun, pleated by hard work and hardship.
With arthritic finger she beckoned him to sit with her.
They shared stories in common tongue
and she read the lines on his hand, a hand unused to toil.
She asked if he would take her picture.

With his assent, she tucked loose strands
beneath her *non la,* smoothed the folds of her *ao dai,*
and lifted the lines on her face with a smile.
Head atilt, eyes bright with the fire of a younger self,
she posed—a frail, old woman transformed.

Mekong Magic

His paddle cleanly slices
The still green water of
Mekong's narrow channel.

Toothless man at canoe's helm,
Safari helmet atop his head,
Sighs with water's song:

Dip, drip, sigh,
Dip, drip, sigh.

Mosquitos buzz, cicadas serenade.
Strangers to the land,
We stay silent, listen to its music.

Dip, drip, sigh,
Dip, drip, sigh.

Might in old man's muscled arms
Surprises us as he
Pulls canoe onto shore.

We tramp deep in jungle
To reach village,
Centuries unchanged.

Residents smile in greeting,
Faces creased by years of toil,
Fortune measured in coconuts.

Sahara Sojourn

Our jeep jostles through a sea of sand
jumping dune waves sculpted by wind
in geometric designs,
sheered, sliced razor sharp,
pocked with perfect round holes
under a cloudless azure sky.

Black tents rise out of the dunes.
Hand woven runners, like red carpets
line the sand leading to each.
Undisturbed by the afternoon heat,
turbaned Berber men draped in royal blue
lift us onto camels as we head
to watch sun set.

Sated from meal of tagine and couscous,
we head to our tent homes for sleep.
Midday's warmth leaves us unprepared
for the ice cold of desert night.

Waking with the City

How I love when Florence wakes and
we share the day's beginning together.

I walk on stones polished by centuries of wear
as I sip my cappuccino and watch the moon

give up his seat to sun as she rises behind me
lighting buildings birthed in Middle Ages.

I check out recently shined shop windows
as street lamps blow out like birthday candles.

The Duomo, looming large, preens for me,
Showing off her white and green marble stripes.

I wave as I pass, happy to see her before she is
blocked from view by tourists as they pose for pictures.

Statues lining piazzas flex their chiseled muscles
reminding me it's time to plan my day.

On Normandy Beach

Blue clouds over Bayeux drip tears on rows
of crosses and stars standing straight and tall,
stark white against the cemetery's
pristine green lawn.

The Channel's chilly waters now clean and bright,
Sunbeams catching sparkles of sand, can't erase
the blood that has spilled here,
the history—

Overwhelmed,
I cry.

Morning Moon Over Iceland

A low-hanging full moon
illumines me when I draw back the drapes—
not the streak of sunlight I expect
slashing the morning sky.

A dust of cloud passes over her,
a nightshirt coming free.
She's so close I could
touch her face.

She evokes a calm that settles me
after the storm of the day before,
when wind howled, propelled rock,
sent travelers searching for shelter.

Birds that hid in bushes during the storm
now fly free and noisily sing morning reveille.
The moon's glow lights my way out the door.
Time to explore.

West Texas Travels

Arid air blows dust across the desert
dotted with pumpjacks dipping
their beaks in and out of the earth
searching for oil. Wind turbines,
their three arms in synchronized dance,
spin to breeze's beat.

Purple sage, an occasional mesquite,
yucca and prickly pear cactus
pepper the barren landscape.
Mountains rise in tall striated columns
thrust through earth by volcanic boil
to form their range.

Those living on this unforgiving territory
crave distance from cities and crowds.
Like the cracked desert earth,
they're crusty on the outside
but their smiles are warm and eyes twinkle
as they ask where we travelers are from.

Dustin tells us the best place for lunch—he's
a cowboy everyone seems to know,
and Luis, the hardware store owner in Presidio
stops us on the street, takes us to his store,
shows us his high school yearbook,
and recounts his family's history.

In Terlingua, Bill plugged a leak in our van's tire
asking for nothing other than our paying
the kindness forward. While folks live
far from others, their cooperative spirit
binds them. They consider where they live
the real Texas.

Tarmac

This was not a day of earned sweat from a rigorous hike,
Or one of happy exhaustion from running around
after grandchildren,
but a day closeted in an airport on uncomfortable chairs,
breathing stale air tainted with fuel fumes.
A day when after many delays we finally boarded the plane
only to sit again—this time on the tarmac.

There was no flight.
We taxied back to the terminal—
weather prohibiting take-off.
This was a day.

Part 7:

Wonders to know

What Is Perfect?

Unblemished peach,
Still stemmed and leaved,
The color of ripe,
Golden skin of fuzz.

The smell of rain
not yet arrived,
Clouds gathering dark,
Earth's drink in wait.

My husband's gaze
on my aging form,
Beaming love as true
as when young, in bloom.

A mother's smile
on my daughter's face
as she holds with pride
her newborn babe.

Baby boy born
but months before,
Eyes round with wonder
at each new day,
Grandson mine
YOU'RE perfect!

Joy in Present Tense

Be in the present, I'm told.
Don't look behind
Don't look ahead
Appreciate the now.

Difficult for one who
tries to understand the past,
Makes plans, sets goals,
Is nourished by achievement.

But now I see a different world
through my grandson's eyes,
Whose wonder at the color of the sky,
The sound of his own laugh,
The texture of his mother's shirt,
All amaze and fascinate him.

He is ever in the present,
Each new day a gift.
He teaches me.

Child of My Child

I cradle the child of my child in my arms,
Her silken newborn hair tickles
As she moves head, twitches limbs,
Mimics moves made in mother's womb
Before deciding to break free.

Caressing her pristine body with my aging skin
I notice the wrinkles on us both.
While mine continue to deepen,
Hers will fill with mother's milk
Creating chipmunk cheeks, Buddha belly.

Can she sense the love in my touch?
See the happiness in my smile?
Hear my heart sing, feel its warmth
As I rock her to sleep, quiet her cries,
Croon as she takes bottle with gusto?

Eyes just now focusing, fingers reaching
She's like Columbus discovering a new world.
I yearn to explore, learn along with her,
To lift the jaded filter from my eyes and
Blink to see the world anew through hers.

Lev's Hands

An outline of my grandson's hands
hangs in portrait on the refrigerator door.
I keep it at his height so he can
see it when he visits.

I brace myself for the day he says,
"Grandma, why do you keep that
silly picture I drew when I was a baby?"
I'll tell him, "Because you drew it for me."

Loving What She Sees

Sitting squatted on her haunches
as only a two-year-old can do,
she peers at herself in full-length mirror.

Perfect round face, dimpled chin and cheeks,
dark eyes bordered by thick black lashes,
eyebrows almost touching.

She sweeps untamable chestnut hair
from one side of her face, then the other.
Pleased, she purses rosebud lips
and sails an air kiss to her mirrored self.

Turning, she sees me watching
and sends me an unselfconscious smile.
I pray when at nine, eleven, fifteen years
and more, she's just as happy with her reflection.

Questions

He's four years old, and bursting with questions.
"How do magnets work?"
"Why is the grass green?"

I fire up my memory chip
stored from long ago—or just yesterday
to form my response . . .

Then I anxiously check his face
for a sign that translates,
"I get it, Grandma."

Eliana at Three

She walks with a bop to her step
And runs with a skip and a hop.
There must be a tune in her head
As her arms do a flip and a flop.

She sings with reckless abandon,
Makes words up as she goes along,
Belts out of tune, but no matter,
Volume is key to her song.

When thinking, brow knits in a bow,
Arms laced across chest 'til it hits
Which book she wants you to read,
Then wriggling beside you she sits.

A cherub with dark, curly mop,
Bright eyes above cheeks all aglow,
She's a bundle of joy overflowing,
Treasure to love, wonder to know.

Koala Hug

His small arms wrap around my neck and
his legs around my waist.
My grandson clutches me the way a koala bear hugs a tree.
His head, tucked between my chin and shoulder,
Leaves his ear available for my whispered,
"I love you."

What would you like for lunch, little miss?

Monkey toes with an alligator nose
would make a delicious dish.

Or would you prefer elephant knees
along with a bowl of green peas?

Perhaps turtle soup with a little shrimp
to give your bread someplace to dip?

Or how about a few kangaroo tails
served with a plate of slimy black snails?

What's that you say—
PB and J?

Is THAT what you'd like for lunch today?

’Twas the First Night of Chanukah

’Twas the first night of Chanukah and through every room
You could smell latkes frying, their taste on the loom.
The menorah was placed in the window with care,
In hopes all would see bright lights shining there.

The children spun dreidels and sang Ma-o-tzur,
Then Grandma and Papa walked through the door.
They had presents for Lev and others for Eli,
But first come the latkes—feast for the belly.

We all sang the prayer, Mama lit the shamash,
Aba played ukulele, children grabbed a nosh.
The first candle was lit, time to open a present,
There’s an Amazon box, let’s see what’s in it.

PJs for Eli, activity book for Lev,
Let’s read a story before time for bed.
Snuggled under covers they sleep through the night,
Dreaming “seven more days”—a child’s delight!

Pick Up at P.S. 261

Like a well-orchestrated stage performance
set to the music of children's laughter,
each class takes its appointed space in the schoolyard.
Young students score a spot on the grass
while older ones cluster around them.
Teachers stand sentry.

Outside a chain link fence wait parents,
grandparents, nannies, and younger siblings.
All look for their charges through
the diamond-shaped spaces in the fence.
Some have their fingers laced through the wire
shouting "Alex," "Lumi," over here "Ali."

At 2:42 the fence gate swings open.
The chaperones flood the schoolyard
like water flowing through a slot canyon.
With child in hand, they exit
by a gate on the opposite side of the yard
and spill onto the street to a chorus of goodbyes.

As I put my arms around my grandson—
my responsibility this day,
I can't help but think what would happen
if a person with a gun and vengeance on his mind
should show up at pick-up time.

Mirror Images

He stands on step stool post-shower,
towel wrapped 'round his
thin body, wet hair matted,
long dark lashes clumped by water,
two large front teeth awaiting braces,
and eyes himself in the bathroom mirror.

I stand next to him as we speak
to the large looking glass.
"I can see why people say
my sister looks like me."
"Maybe around the eyes," I tell him.
"You look very like your mother, though."

He asks me who I look like.
I tell him our faces often change over the years.
"When I was young, I looked like my father. Now
when I look in the mirror, I see my mother."
"When *I* look in the mirror," says he,
"I see myself!"

Part 8:

Dance

Paradigm Shift

Where once the thought of living in Florida
was anathema
and envisioning myself a retiree
impossible,
I now live among palms on its west coast.

I feel I'm living someone else's life—
someone who can pick up a book,
travel, write, or take a dip in the pool
if and when she wants.

Gears ground slowly, squeakily,
Reaching the point where
I could accept this slower pace,
Live with less structure.

Good news came with the change—
the gift of time.
Grateful for the view
through this new lens.

Waiting for . . .

my first day of school
summer vacation
my birthday to roll around

college acceptance letter
the call to say I landed the job
that special someone to love

the start of a family
our child to find her footing
grandchildren to spoil

my husband's surgeon to say,
"You can see him now."

Mother's Day

I wonder what my daughter thinks as she watches us age—
Father looking like her grandfather as he carries
her three-year-old son tentatively into the ocean,
Mother taking so much time getting up
from the sand where she plays with baby sister.

I wonder what my daughter thinks as she watches us age—
My stature shorter, his more stooped,
Both more set in our ways, moving more slowly
through days we try not to jam-pack
and nights when we hope sleep comes easily.

This year, a Mother's Day card with the message:
I am strong because a strong woman raised me.
Inside the card my daughter wrote, "Thank you for being a
constant source of strength and influence throughout my life."
Spirit is ageless.

Rockaway Beach at 108th Street

I can see my grandmother lifting her skirt at the shore,
Bathing bare feet, breathing in the salt air with eyes closed,
Her version of meditation, her medicine.

Mother, too, drew strength from the ocean.
I remember her in white bathing cap, waves lapping at her legs,
her waist unlikely to taste the sea.
Eventually, she would watch waves from her wheelchair.

The beach is an elixir for me.
My mind, always spinning, slows to the beat of poetry
as the ocean's sounds quells worries
leaving me free to make the important decision
to jump over or duck under a wave.

Now a new generation enjoys these waters.
My daughter and her children romp at Rockaway,
A routine that involves castles and moats,
peanut butter sandwiches and ice cream treats,
wave chasing and jumping with their father holding tight.

Can memories wash in on a wave?

I have my answer.

Good Morning

I remember when morning's first light
slipped beneath window's shade
I'd throw back the sheet, bounce from bed,
and greet the day head on.

Now I work at pushing away
the night's thick fog.
Eyelids resist,
still heavy with sleep and dream.

My limbs creak
as I make my way out of bed
to the kitchen
and my coffee pot.

Serena

We met on the studio dance floor,
She, a teacher in her prime, I a student
entering life's last third.
Her movement, music, and joy
placed a magic spell on the space.

Years of Covid isolation ensued,
the studio went up in flames,
Serena moved away, taking her gift
along with the delight
it brought me.

But we've found each other once again.
She now smiles from a computer screen
and asks me to "step in" with her.
I do, and with leaps and sways, I
dance on my bedroom carpet.

She leaves me beaming, sweaty,
heart open, spirits lifted,
serene.

Crash!

No clang of metal on metal,
No whiplash to the body,
No blood, no sound
accompanies this crash.

Only silence, blackness,
a blank screen that stares at me.
Moments ago my words
were projected on her.

At first I thought she was toying with me,
reminding me who was boss.
So I clicked keys that in the past
resurrected her, but had no luck.

Filled with fear and dread for the loss
of work painstakingly created,
and the messages yet to be read,
I pushed myself away to think.

Helpless, held hostage to her,
I wonder who to call, lean on for support.
While I ponder, I hear a ding
and a request for my password appears.

My world is set right again.
But she's told me she's tired,
Old, not unlike me.
Perhaps it's time to part ways.

I need a new computer.
She needs a younger master.

Field of Lost Words

My lost words laze and graze
in faraway field,
Blown there, flown there,
Leaving my story with no end,
Joke with no punch,
Friend with no name.

Some words are lost forever,
Others are lifted from their lair,
blown back to me by stiff breeze
in night's wee hours when no one
hears me say,
"That's the word I was looking for!"

Every year my field of lost words
grows by acres.
I fear one day I'll realize
it's not my words that are lost—
I am.

L'Dor V'Dor

from Generation to Generation

I see my daughter in the thick of it,
And marvel at the speed with which she
Spins 'round kitchen, whips up dinner,
Engages toddler, answers texts, changes diaper.
I'm exhausted just watching, feeling in the way.
I wonder how she manages to balance it all—
Work, family, with strength and bright spirit.

Was I once able to do that too?
Yes, when I was in the thick of it—
A career to build, a marriage to cultivate,
A child to nurture, a home to create.

My days seem thinner now.
Seems like too little to do,
and it takes too long
to do the doing.

Tough to accept, but I'm
learning to dance to
a slower beat, to
sit back, and
enjoy the
thinning
of time.

Take a Breath

Stop the words now.
Open the window in the centre of your chest
And let the spirits fly out.

—Rumi

If I open the window of my chest and let the air out,
Will I feel freer,
loosen muscles to listen more acutely,
be more amenable to change,
make more room for beauty,
dance to a new song,
make peace with growing old?

Life's Song

At times I think how pleasant it'd be,
If life's song were written in the key of C.
No sharps creating anxious peaks,
No flats to sound the lows.

But how boring life'd be then.
No rankle or jangle of dissonant chords,
Or thrill of trill by keys black and white.
So I'll keep my song as written,

Live with keyboard's ups and downs.
I'll throw in some playful harmonies,
Peaceful choruses as well, and
Enjoy each year of music 'til the final swell.

Missing My Warwick Friend

We met by chance when our lives upended,
By choice we became fast friends.
Not a character in each other's history,
We felt free to share whole truths,
Filling a void for the other
around your kitchen table.

Like you, your poetry was sensuous,
Words your heart felt spilled on the page,
Poems of lovers and loves lost, stories of a life
full of joy, heartache.

Designing a home on a shoestring, your métier.
You could slice a table in half, attach it to a wall,
and it worked, warm one of your rooms
with a discarded rug.

Lee, I miss seeing your mop of dark curls
bounce with your laugh and
your bright, red-rimmed smile—
lipstick the same scarlet as your nails.

I think of you
When choosing a paint color,
When I want to share something unsharable,
When I want to hear your deep, throaty laugh,
When I feel guilty about moving away
leaving you and Warwick behind,
When I remember you passed
without my being there to say good-bye.

Ochs Orchard

The clock's hands spin backward
as we wind our way up the road—
once dirt and rutted, now paved—
to reach my favorite hilltop.

Here sits Ochs Farmstand and Orchard.
From this vantage point I can
gaze at the valley below—the valley
my home for much of my life.

The Ochs family still owns this site where
the tick tock of time would take a break
and I'd linger, close to the clouds,
to ponder life's big questions.

I miss this calm, contemplative space
and the community where neighbors
worked together to care for
the place we called home.

My Mind's Museum

The galleries of my mind's museum
are crammed.
I have to rotate my holdings
so more recent memories
move to the rear,
past ones now front and center.

Scenes from childhood, images
of family long gone, replace
yesterday's happenings,
today's events.

I wonder where I'll find room for my dreams—
musings of a future still in need of
brushstrokes, color, light, and frames.
I hope a new wing is in the works.

Notes

In "The Photographer and the Vietnamese Woman," the term "*non la*" refers to a type of Vietnamese headwear (conical hat) used to shield the face from sun and rain. The term "*ao dai*" in the poem refers to the traditional dress of Vietnamese women—a long tunic with slits on either side of wide trousers.

About the Author

Judith Rosner's poetry appears in a number of literary journals, including *HerWords, The City Key, The Jewish Literary Journal, The Naugatuck River Review,* and in print and online anthologies.

While she's written and published personal essays earlier in life, she came to poetry in her mid-sixties. She woke one morning with a poem in her head and hasn't stopped writing them since. She enjoys the challenge of creating a piece with few words that carries the weight of many and finds connection with others through her poetry.

She holds a Ph.D. in Sociology and retired first from a career as college professor, and then from her firm The Rosner Group, a training and consulting company that specialized in leadership development and executive coaching. She and her husband split their time between Sarasota, Florida and New York City.

www.ingramcontent.com/pod-product-compliance
Lightning Source LLC
LaVergne TN
LVHW091813110826
845146LV00006B/989

* 9 7 9 8 9 0 1 4 6 9 0 4 0 *